# THE ASSASSINATION OF JFK: 11/22/63

## Taylor Sapp

Alphabet Publishing

www.AlphabetPublish.com

He was one of the United States' most popular presidents, shot and killed during a typical campaign event in a motorcade parade. His killer, a lone gunman with a mysterious background...or simply the face of a conspiracy that could have involved foreign powers, organized crime, and possibly even the US government?

# INTRODUCTION

John Fitzgerald "Jack" Kennedy (May 29, 1917 – November 22, 1963), commonly referred to by his initials JFK, was an American politician who served as the 35th President of the United States from January 1961 until his assassination in November 1963, a day still shrouded in mystery and conspiracy to this day.

## Introductory Questions

1. Have you ever heard of John F. Kennedy?
2. What do you know about John F. Kennedy?
3. Do you know of any famous people that were assassinated?
4. What does the word *conspiracy* mean to you?
5. What do you think this famous quote by JFK from his inaugural address at winning the presidency means? "Ask not what your country can do for you, ask what you can do for your country."
6. What else do you know about JFK? Can you think of anything important he did?
7. What do you know about any other U.S. Presidents? What is one important thing they did?

# CONTENTS

# BIOGRAPHY

John Fitzgerald Kennedy, also known as JFK, was a famous and influential US president who was born on May 29, 1917 in Brookline, Massachusetts. He came from a rich and powerful family and went to Harvard University where he did well in school.

Kennedy while serving as Ensign in the U.S. Navy

After college, JFK joined the Navy during World War II and helped save his crew when their boat was attacked by the enemy. After the war, he got into politics and became a Congressman and then a Senator. In 1960, he ran for president as a Democrat and won against a Republican named Richard Nixon. His famous inauguration speech said that people should focus on helping their country instead of just themselves.

Inauguration, 20 Jan. 1961

Kennedy, his wife Jacqueline, and children Caroline and John Jr.

As President, JFK had to deal with problems both inside and outside of the United States. He worked hard to make sure everyone was treated fairly and he also made good choices when it came to other countries.

Tragically, JFK's life was cut short on November 22, 1963 when he was assassinated while riding in a motorcade in Dallas, Texas. His death shocked the nation and the world, leaving a legacy of hope, inspiration, and the question of what might have been.

## JFK'S FINAL TRAGIC DAY

It was a cloudy morning on Friday, November 22, 1963. A big crowd of supporters was waiting outside the Fort Worth Texas Hotel where the President and his wife had stayed the night before. The President came out to give a short speech and shake hands with the audience. He talked about important issues and achievements like the military and space exploration, and thanked the people of Texas for all their support. Then he and his wife got in a convertible to go to Dallas for another event.

Kennedy's limousine in Dallas, before the shooting

As they were driving through Dealey Plaza in the president's motorcade, shots suddenly rang out. The President and Governor were both hit by bullets and rushed to the hospital.

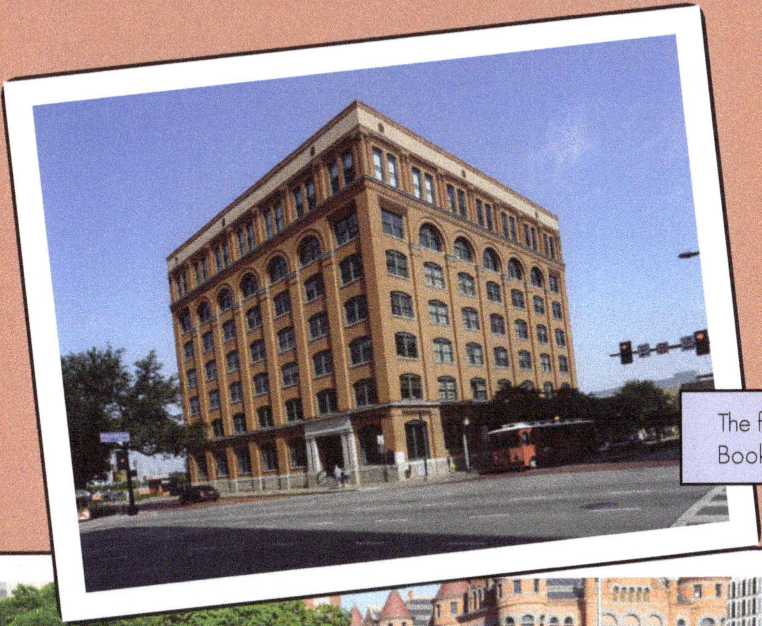

The former Texas Book Depository

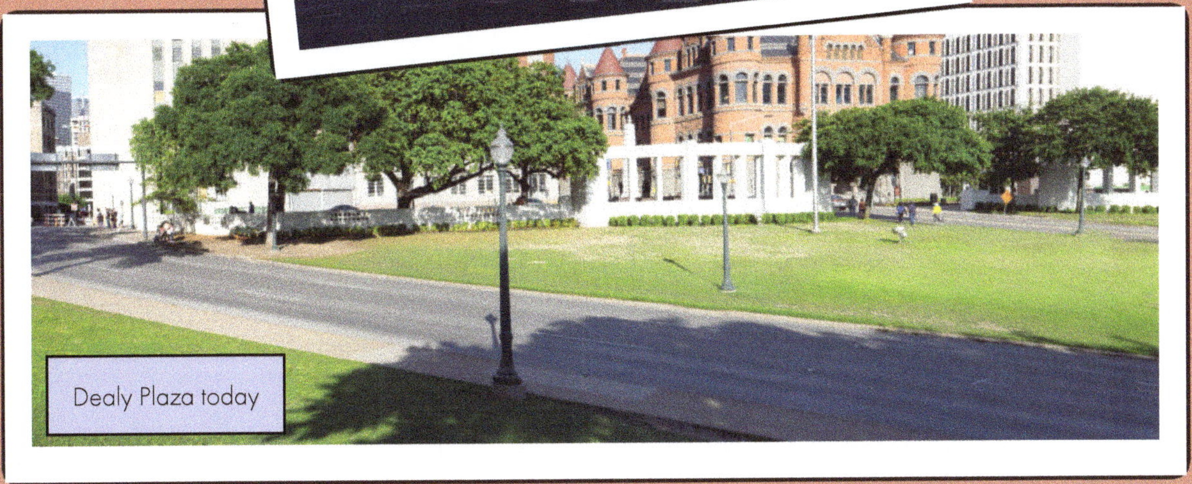

Dealy Plaza today

Map of Dealy Plaza on November 22, 1963

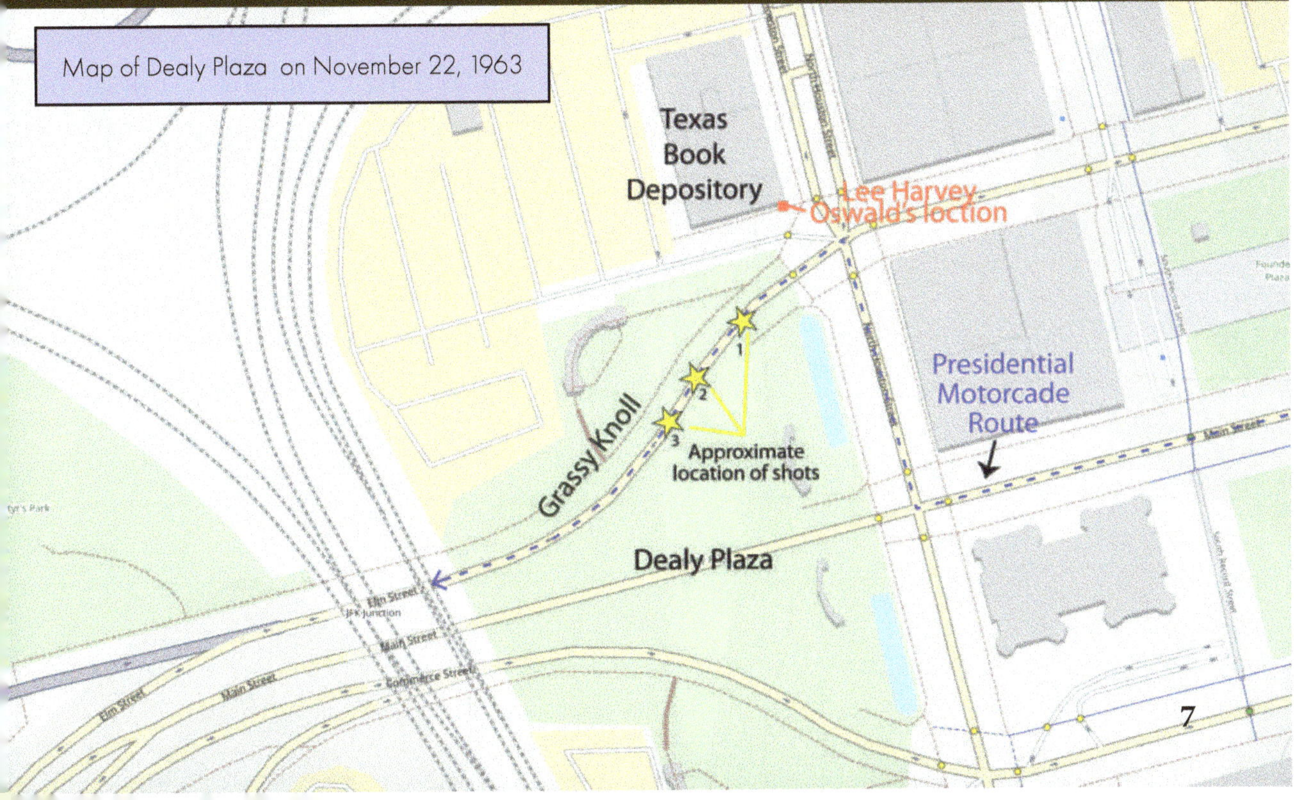
Texas
Book
Depository
Lee Harvey
Oswald's loction
Presidential
Motorcade
Route
1
2
3
Approximate
location of shots
Grassy Knoll
Dealy Plaza
Elm Street
Main Street
Commerce Street

Loading the coffin on to Air Force One

Vice President Johnson sworn in

Jack Ruby at his arrest

Sadly, the President did not survive, but the Governor would recover from his injuries.

Lee Harvey Oswald, the man who shot the President was arrested, but two days later another man named Jack Ruby shot him before he could go to trial. This added more confusion to an already sad and mysterious event.

The assassination led to immediate shock and confusion, with the nation and the world shocked with the news of the president's death. The president's body was brought to Love Field and placed on Air Force One.

Before the plane took off, Vice President Lyndon B. Johnson stood in the crowded compartment of Air Force One and took the oath of office, administered by the US District Court.

# LEE HARVEY OSWALD

PHOTOGRAPH OF LEE HARVEY OSWALD AT ABOUT TIME OF HIS DEFECTION

On November 22, 1963 at 2:15 p.m., a 24 year old man named Lee Harvey Oswald was arrested for shooting and killing President John F. Kennedy and police officer J.D. Tippit. According to the official investigation, Oswald acted alone. He fired three shots from a sixth-floor window at the southeast corner of the Book Depository where he had also been working.

Just two days later, on November 24, Oswald was shot and killed by another man named Jack Ruby on TV. This added to the mystery surrounding his life and death.

Oswald had a difficult childhood, with his father dying before he was born and spending time in orphanages. He joined the Marines and went to the Soviet Union for a few years before returning to America with his wife and daughter. He got into trouble for trying to assassinate General Edwin A. Walker in 1963 and traveling to communist countries. During questioning, Oswald denied being involved in the assassination, saying he was just used as a patsy.

Oswald as a Marine

According to one writer, Oswald didn't hate Kennedy personally but hated the American system and its ideas of capitalism, so he targeted the President as a symbol of that system.

In an interview with *Frontline*, investigative journalist Gerald Posner said Oswald's hatred wasn't for Kennedy. "What he did hate was the system and what Kennedy

stood for," Posner tells the PBS show. "He despised America. He despised capitalism. When he eventually had the opportunity to strike against Kennedy, it was the symbol of the system that he was going after."

The brief ceremony took place at 2:38 p.m. before the plane departed from Dallas.

On November 25, a horse-drawn carriage carried Kennedy's flag-draped coffin to St. Matthew's Catholic Cathedral from the Capitol Rotunda. More than 800,000 people lined Pennsylvania Avenue to watch the procession.

Caroline and John Jr. Kennedy riding in the funeral procession

The funeral procession leaving the White House

# TIMELINE OF JFK'S TRAGIC DAY

**November 22nd**
**~12:30 p.m. CST**: President Kennedy's motorcade enters Dealey Plaza in Dallas, Texas as he travels with his wife, Jacqueline Kennedy; Texas Governor John Connally; and Connally's wife, Nellie Connally.

**12:30 p.m.** Gunshots ring out as the motorcade passes through Dealey Plaza. President Kennedy is struck by two bullets, one in the upper back and one in the head. Governor Connally is also hit by a bullet.

**~12:34 p.m.** The motorcade rushes to Parkland Memorial Hospital, where President Kennedy is pronounced dead at 1:00 p.m. CST.

**~12:40 p.m.** Lee Harvey Oswald, a former Marine and the presumed assassin, leaves the Texas School Book Depository where he worked.

**1:15 p.m.** Dallas Police Officer J.D. Tippit is fatally shot by Lee Harvey Oswald in the Oak Cliff neighborhood of Dallas.

**~1:45 p.m.** Oswald is arrested at the Texas Theatre in Oak Cliff after being spotted by a movie theater employee who recognized him from a police description.

**2:38 p.m.** Vice President Lyndon B. Johnson is sworn in as the 36th President of the United States aboard Air Force One before it departs from Dallas.

**November 23rd**: Johnson declares November 25th a national day of remembering JFK.

**November 24th**: Lee Harvey Oswald is shot and killed by Jack Ruby, a local nightclub owner, while in police custody at the Dallas Police Department. Oswald dies at Parkland Memorial Hospital at 1:07 p.m. CST.

Kennedy was buried with full military honors at Arlington National Cemetery with leaders from dozens of nations in attendance. Jacqueline Kennedy lit an eternal flame at his grave site that has continued to shine since JFK's death.

Graves of JFK, Jacqueline Kennedy Onassis, and two of their children, Patrick (died as a baby) and Arabella Kennedy (died stillborn)

Shortly after President Kennedy was tragically killed on November 22, 1963, President Lyndon B. Johnson set up a group called the Warren Commission to find out what had happened. The commission's job was to look into the assassination of President Kennedy and the killing of the man accused of doing it, Lee Harvey Oswald, and make a report with their findings. According to their investigation, Oswald did everything alone. He shot three times from a sixth-floor window in a building called the Book Depository.

# THE SINGLE BULLET THEORY

The single bullet, image from the
National Archive

The term "single bullet theory" is used to explain how President John F. Kennedy was killed. The theory says that one bullet hit Kennedy in the back and then also hit Texas Governor John Connally. This bullet was supposedly fired by Lee Harvey Oswald from the Texas Book Depository. It entered Kennedy's back, exited through his throat, and then hit Connally's chest, wrist, and thigh. The bullet was later found on a stretcher at the hospital.

This theory is important because it supports what the Warren Commission believed—that Oswald acted alone. Some people don't believe this theory because they think the bullet couldn't have caused all the injuries it did and still stay almost whole. Skeptics call it the "magic bullet theory"! But even with these doubts, the single bullet theory is still a big part of the official explanation for JFK's assassination and is talked about by many people today also connected to a possible conspiracy.

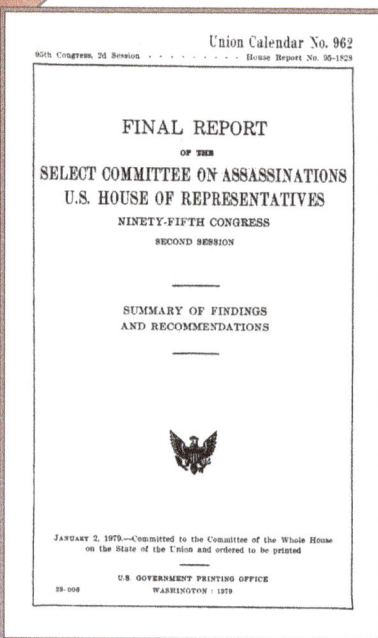

But some people weren't convinced by this report. In 1976, another group called the House Select Committee on Assassinations (HSCA) was created. They released a report in 1979 that said there was "probably" more than one person involved in Kennedy's death but they couldn't figure out who or why. This conclusion was based on different pieces of evidence like recordings of gunshots and looking into a man named Jack Ruby. But scientists disagreed on the sound evidence and we still don't have all the answers today!

Even though the official report says Oswald acted alone, many people believe he didn't or that others helped him—maybe bad guys, the government, or people from Cuba. A survey done in 2017 found that only about one third of Americans think Oswald was the only one responsible for killing Kennedy.

## LEARN MORE

John F. Kennedy Presidential Library and Museum: https://www.jfklibrary.org/

JFK Assassination Records, National Archives and Records Administration: https://www.archives.gov/research/jfk/release-2025

Assassination of John F. Kennedy. Wikipedia: https://en.wikipedia.org/wiki/Assassination_of_John_F._Kennedy

John F. Kennedy, Wikipedia: https://en.wikipedia.org/wiki/John_F._Kennedy

In recent years, thousands of documents that had never been seen before were released by the National Archive. A large release was made in March of 2025 that included unedited versions of previously released documents. Still the mystery remains.

The assassination of President Kennedy led to lots of investigations, theories, and arguments about how he died. Official reports like the Warren Commission say Oswald was the only one involved but this is still disputed and we may never know for sure what really happened as alternative theories persist to this day.

## HOW HEALTH ISSUES IMPACTED JFK IN LIFE AND DEATH

While John F. Kennedy was the youngest person ever elected to the Oval Office at 43, his health was a consistent issue throughout most of his life. Outwardly, he seemed healthy. The American public didn't know that he struggled with numerous health issues.

Despite JFK's slim, athletic-looking physique and love of sports and outdoor activities like golf and sailing, he had to deal with spinal problems and osteoporosis that left him in chronic pain. He was also afflicted with Addison's Disease, a condition that causes fatigue, digestive difficulties, and low blood pressure. In addition, he experienced severe allergies and urinary tract infections as well. There are theories that even if JFK had lived, he might not have had to leave office at some point due to his health issues.

Finally, JFK's major back issues are believed to have impacted what happened when he was shot in 1963. Dr. John Lattimer, a physician expert on the assassination, was the first non-government official to review autopsy photographs and clothing. He believes the president may have survived if not for his tightly bound back brace. The brace could have returned him to an upright position after the first gunshot hit his back. The theory stresses that if not for the brace, Kennedy might have fallen forward and remained out of the line of fire for the second, fatal shot.

## Oswald didn't act alone

The single (or "magic") bullet theory critics argue that the bullet's trajectory and the extent of the damage it caused make it unlikely to have caused all the injuries attributed to it. This single bullet is the second of two bullets alleged to have hit JFK and one of three fired by Oswald in total.

Additionally, skeptics question whether a single bullet could have remained largely intact after causing such extensive damage.

## The mafia did it

They had him killed because Kennedy was unsuccessful in overthrowing Fidel Castro in Cuba, meaning mafia-run casinos there remained shutdown.

Robert Kennedy, the President's brother, was also cracking down on the mob in his role as attorney general. He was pursuing a case against Jimmy Hoffa, a union leader suspected of being involved with organized crime. Robert himself would be assassinated only 5 years later

## The US government was involved

Some rogue element in the CIA could have been angry over the unsuccessful Bay of Pigs invasion in Cuba. This attempted coup of Communist dictator Fidel Castro and his government was an embarrassing military failure for US intelligence and JFK was blamed at some for not providing appropriate support.

Some government officials may have been concerned about Kennedy pulling out of the Vietnam War.

# WHY DOES IT MATTER?

JFK's assassination marked the beginning of our modern era of conspiracy theories that continues to this day, as seen with the many COVID-related conspiracy claims. Conspiracy theorists often have distrust in the government and doubt the official stories of many important events. Here are just five of many examples that have taken place in the USA and abroad since JFK's assassination:

## Famous Conspiracies Theories

### 1. Moon Landing Hoax (1969)

**Theory**: Some people believe the Apollo moon landings were staged by NASA with the help of Hollywood, as part of a Cold War space race propaganda effort.

**Claim**: The footage was filmed on a sound stage, and various anomalies like the flag waving or inconsistent shadows are cited as "proof."

### 2. Watergate Scandal (1972-1974)

**Theory**: While the Watergate scandal led to President Nixon's resignation, conspiracy theorists believe it was just the tip of a larger iceberg of government corruption and cover-ups involving multiple agencies and secret operations beyond what was revealed.

**Claim**: The break-in was part of a broader strategy involving deeper conspiracies between political operatives and intelligence agencies.

### 3. Iran-Contra Affair (1980s)

**Theory**: The U.S. government was secretly involved in illegal arms sales to Iran and funneling money to Nicaraguan Contras despite public denials and legal prohibitions. The full extent of CIA involvement remains a subject of speculation.

**Claim**: Some believe the affair was a small part of a much larger network of clandestine operations run by the U.S. to influence foreign governments.

## 4. 9/11 Attacks (2001)

**Theory**: Numerous conspiracy theories emerged in the wake of the September 11th terrorist attacks, with claims that the U.S. government, or elements within it, either orchestrated the attacks or allowed them to happen.

**Claim**: The collapse of the World Trade Center towers, particularly Building 7, has fueled theories that the buildings were brought down by controlled demolition, not planes.

## 5. COVID-19 Pandemic (2020)

**Theory**: Various conspiracy theories emerged around the origins and handling of the COVID-19 pandemic, ranging from it being a bioweapon to a coordinated effort by governments to impose social control.

**Claim**: The virus was engineered or deliberately released, or that the pandemic is being used as a pretext for mass surveillance or forced vaccinations.

# INTERESTING FACTS

Claims and misinformation about JFK's assassination continue to this day. As recently as the 2020 election, Republican candidate and President Donald J. Trump even accused his competitor Ted Cruz's father of being involved in the JFK Assassination!

JFK's Assassination has been fodder for lots of famous media, including:

*The Trial of Lee Harvey Oswald* (1977) — This made-for-TV movie imagines what would have happened if Lee Harvey Oswald had survived and gone to trial for Kennedy's assassination.

Oliver Stone's film's *JFK* (1991) — This film details many of the conspiracy theories about the assassination. This film is one of the most famous dramatizations of the assassination. It follows New Orleans District Attorney Jim Garrison as he investigates a conspiracy behind Kennedy's death, suggesting involvement from various government agencies. The movie sparked renewed public interest in the assassination and pushed for the release of classified government documents.

In popular science fiction, the idea of being able to change the past has been depicted in many forms such as the famous novel (and TV limited series) 11/22/63 by Stephen King is about Jake Epping, a high school teacher who finds a way to travel back in time to 1958. His mission is to stop the assassination of President John F. Kennedy on November 22, 1963. The story explores whether changing the past is worth the risk and the impact it has on the present and Jake's life. It's a mix of history, time travel, and love.

# GLOSSARY

**achievements** (n.) — successful things done with skill; accomplishments

**approximately** (adv.) — around, almost, exact (often used with time)

**assassinated** (n.) — murdered

**convertible** (n.) — a car with an open top

**conspiracy** (n.) —  secret plan by a group to do something unlawful or harmful

**disputed** (v) — something that many disagree about

**fatally** (adv.) — causing death

**influential** (adj) — greatly listened to and followed to by others

**motorcade** (n.) — a parade of cars

**patsy** (n.) — a person cheated or blamed for something

# DISCUSSION QUESTIONS

1. Why do you think a lone gunman like Lee Harvey Oswald would want to kill JFK?

2. Why do lone killers sometimes want to kill famous or important people?

3. Compare the conspiracy theories about JFK's assassination.

4. Which seems the most likely?

5. Which seems the most unlikely?

6. Do you think JFK was an important American president?

7. What other American presidents do you think were important? Why?

8. Do you know of any other political assassinations in history? In your own country or area?

9. How can leaders be protected from assassination?

10. Has it become easier or more difficult to protect leaders in the modern age? Why do you think so?

# INVESTIGATING THE JFK ASSASSINATION: A WEBQUEST

**Introduction:**

Welcome, investigators! In this webquest, you will delve into one of the most significant events in American history: the assassination of President John F. Kennedy. Your task is to explore various aspects of the assassination, examine different theories, and analyze evidence to form your conclusions about what truly happened on that fateful day in Dallas.

**Task:**

1.  Your mission is to investigate the assassination of President John F. Kennedy and answer the following questions:

2.  What were the key events leading up to the assassination?

3.  What happened on November 22, 1963, in Dealey Plaza, Dallas, Texas?

4.  What evidence exists to support different theories about the assassination?

5.  What are the main theories surrounding the assassination, and what evidence supports or refutes each theory?

6.  What impact did the assassination of JFK have on American society and politics?

**Process:**

Begin your investigation by familiarizing yourself with the events leading up to the assassination. Use reputable sources such as history textbooks or educational websites to gain an understanding of JFK's presidency, his policies, and the political climate of the time.

Explore primary sources, such as eyewitness testimonies, photographs, and videos, to learn about what transpired on November 22, 1963, in Dealey Plaza. You can find these primary sources in archives, museums, or online databases.

Examine different theories surrounding the assassination, including the lone gunman theory, the conspiracy theories involving multiple shooters, and the CIA or Mafia involvement theories. Evaluate the evidence for each theory and consider the credibility of the sources presenting them.

Analyze the impact of the assassination on American society and politics. Look into how JFK's death affected public trust in government institutions, led to changes in security measures for public officials, and influenced subsequent presidential administrations.

## Resources:

- National Archives: JFK Assassination Records Collection: www.archives.gov/research/jfk
- John F. Kennedy Presidential Library and Museum: www.jfklibrary.org
- The Sixth Floor Museum at Dealey Plaza: www.jfk.org
- PBS: American Experience—JFK: www.pbs.org/wgbh/americanexperience/features/kennedys-bio-john-fitzgerald/
- History.com: John F. Kennedy Assassination: www.history.com/search?q=john+f+kennedy+assassination

- *Case Closed: Lee Harvey Oswald and the Assassination of JFK* by Gerald Posner
- *Crossfire: The Plot That Killed Kennedy* by Jim Marrs

## Evaluation:

Your investigation will be assessed based on the depth of your research, the accuracy of your analysis, and the clarity of your conclusions. Make sure to cite your sources properly and present your findings in a coherent manner.

## Conclusion:

Congratulations, investigators, on completing your exploration of the JFK assassination! By examining various perspectives and analyzing evidence, you have gained valuable insights into this pivotal moment in history. Remember, the quest for truth and understanding is ongoing, and your findings contribute to the ongoing dialogue surrounding this significant event.

# REFERENCES

Bomboy, S. (n.d.). What if JFK had Survived his Assassination?—National Constitution Center. National Constitution Center – constitutioncenter.org. https://constitutioncenter.org/blog/what-if-jfk-had-survived-his-assassination/

Halleman, C. (2017, October 26). The Kennedy Conspiracy Theories That Still Endure 50 Years After JFK's Death. Town & Country. https://www.townandcountrymag.com/society/politics/a13093037/jfk-assassination-conspiracy-theories/

History.com Editors. (2009, November 24). President John F. Kennedy is Assassinated. HISTORY. https://www.history.com/this-day-in-history/john-f-kennedy-assassinated

Selverstone, M. (2020, May 27). John F. Kennedy: Domestic Affairs. Miller Center. https://millercenter.org/president/kennedy/domestic-affairs

Addison's disease—Symptoms, Causes, Treatment. (1985). National Organization for Rare Disorders. https://rarediseases.org/rare-diseases/addisons-disease/

Breslow, J. (2021, November 22). 8 Things You May Not Know About Lee Harvey Oswald. FRONTLINE. https://www.pbs.org/wgbh/frontline/article/8-things-you-may-not-know-about-lee-harvey-oswald/

Brown, D. (2017, October 26). The Day John F. Kennedy Was Killed: How America Mourned a Fallen President. The Washington Post. https://www.washingtonpost.com/news/retropolis/wp/2017/10/26/how-america-mourned-john-f-kennedy-images-of-grief-for-a-fallen-president/

Byrne, J. (2023, June 15). The Hours Before Dallas. National Archives. https://www.archives.gov/publications/prologue/2000/summer/jfk-last-day-1

House Select Committee. (1976). House Select Committee on Assassinations (HSCA). JFK Final Assassination Report. https://www.history-matters.com/archive/jfk/hsca/contents.htm

Kiger, P. (2023, May 2). The Health Problems JFK Hid From the Public. HISTORY. https://www.history.com/news/the-health-problems-jfk-hid-from-the-public

Rockwood, B. (1993). Who Was Lee Harvey Oswald? . FRONTLINE. broadcast, PBS.

Warren Commission. (1964). Warren Commission Report. National Archives. https://www.archives.gov/research/jfk/warren-commission-report

ISBN: 978-1-956159-60-8 (print)

For permission requests, write to the publisher at "ATTN: Permissions", at the address below:

29 Milo Dr. Branford, CT 06405 USA
info@alphabetpublishingbooks.com
www.AlphabetPublishingBooks.com

Discounts on class sets and bulk orders available upon inquiry.

Cover and Interior Design by Walton Burns

Country of Manufacture Specified on Last Page

First Printing 2025

## Images

Cover Depositphotos /Jose Carva_683821534 licensed • pg. 1 top left Ancestry Explorer, Public Domain • pg. 1 top right Wikimedia/Cecil Stoughton, Public Domain • pg. 1 bottom right Ancestry Explorer, Public Domain • pg. 1 bottom left Wikimedia, Public Domain • pg. 5 top Wikimedia/Unknown, Public Domain • pg. 5 bottom left JFK Presidential Library /Abbie Rowe, Public Domain • pg. 5 bottom right Robert LeRoy Knudsen, Public Domain • pg. 6 Wikimedia/Walter Sisco, Public Domain • pg. 8 top JFK Presidential Library /Cecil Stoughton, Public Domain • pg. 8 middle Wikimedia/Cecil Stoughton, Public Domain • pg. 8 bottom U.S. National Archives & Records Administration/Unknown, Public Domain • pg. 9 middle U.S. National Archives & Records Administration/ Unknown, Public Domain • pg. 9 bottom JFK Presidential Library /US Marine Corps, Public Domain • pg. 10 left JFK Presidential Library /Cecil Stoughton, Public Domain • pg. 10 right JFK Presidential Library /Robert LeRoy Knudsen, Public Domain • pg. 11 top Wikimedia/Micharl Barera, CC by-SA 4.0 • pg. 11 middle Depositphotos /Alessandro Scagliusi, licensed • pg. 11 bottom OpenStreets Map/edited by Walton Burns, CC by-SA 2.0 • pg. 12 Wikimedia/Acroterion, CC by-SA 4.0 • pg. 13 Wikimedia/HSCA, Public Domain • pg. 14 National Archive/ HSCA, Public Domain • pg. 18 Wikimedia/NASA, Public Domain • pg. 20 left JFK Presidential Library /Cecil Stoughton, Public Domain • pg. 20 right Wikimedia/Matt H. Wade, CC by-SA 3.0